DATE DUE

DEMCO, INC. 38-2931

AN

ACCOUNT

OF THE

SLAVE TRADE

ON THE

COAST OF AFRICA.

———————

AMS PRESS
NEW YORK

AN

ACCOUNT

OF THE

SLAVE TRADE

ON THE

COAST OF AFRICA.

————————————

BY

ALEXANDER FALCONBRIDGE,

LATE SURGEON IN THE AFRICAN TRADE.

————————————

LONDON:

PRINTED BY J. PHILLIPS, GEORGE YARD, LOMBARD-
STREET.

MDCCLXXXVIII.

Library of Congress Cataloging in Publication Data

Falconbridge, Alexander, d. 1792.
An account of the slave trade on the coast of
Africa.

1. Slave-trade--Africa. 2. Slave-trade--
West Indies, British. I. Title.
HT1321.F3 1973   382'.44   77-168002
ISBN 0-404-00255-2

From the edition of 1788, London
First AMS edition published in 1973
Manufactured in the United States of America

AMS PRESS INC.
NEW YORK, N.Y.   10003

PREFACE.

THE following sheets are intended to lay before the public the present state of a branch of the British commerce, which, ever since its existence, has been held in detestation by all good men, but at this time more particularly engages the attention of the nation, and is become the object of general reprobation.

Leaving to abler pens to expatiate more at large on the injustice and inhumanity of the *Slave Trade*, I shall content myself with giving some account of the hardships which the unhappy objects of it undergo, and the cruelties they suffer, from the period of their being reduced to a state of slavery, to their being disposed of in the West India islands; where, I fear, their grievances find little alleviation. At the same time, I shall treat of a subject, which appears not to have been attended to in the manner its importance requires; that is, the sufferings and loss of the seamen employed in this trade; which, from the intemperature of the climate, the inconveniencies they labour under during the voyage, and the severity of most of the commanders, occasion the destruction of great numbers annually.

And this I shall endeavour to do by the recital of a number of facts which have fallen under my own immediate observation, or the knowledge of which I have obtained from persons on whose veracity I can depend.

And happy shall I esteem myself, if an experience obtained by a series of inquiries and observations, made during several voyages to the coast

of

of Africa, shall enable me to render any service to a cause, which is become the cause of every person of humanity.

Before I proceed to the methods of obtaining the slaves, and their subsequent treatment, the treatment of the sailors, and a concise account of the places on the coast of Africa where slaves are obtained, (which I purpose to annex,) it may not be unnecessary to give a short sketch of the usual proceedings of the ships employed in the slave trade.

A N
A C C O U N T
OF THE
SLAVE TRADE, &c.

Proceedings during the Voyage.

ON the arrival of the ships at Bonny, and New Calabar, it is customary for them to unbend the sails, strike the yards and topmasts, and begin to build what they denominate *a house*. This is effected in the following manner. The sailors first lash the booms and yards from mast to mast, in order to form a *ridge-pole.*—About ten feet above the deck, several spars, equal in length to the ridge pole, are next lashed to the standing rigging, and form a wall-plate. Across the ridge-pole and wall-plate, several other spars or rafters are afterwards laid and lashed, at the distance of about six inches from each other. On these, other rafters or spars are laid length-wise, equal in extent to the ridge-pole, so as to form a kind of

lattice

lattice or net-work, with interstices of six inches square. The roof is then covered with mats, made of rushes of very loose texture, fastened together with rope-yarn, and so placed, as to lap over each other like tiles. The space between the deck and the wall-plate, is likewise enclosed with a kind of lattice, or net-work, formed of sticks, lashed acrofs each other, and leaving vacancies of about four inches square. Near the mainmaft, a partition is conftructed of inch deal boards, which reaches athwart the ship. This division is called a *barricado*. It is about eight feet in height, and is made to project near two feet over the sides of the ship. In this barricado there is a door, at which a centinel is placed during the time the negroes are permitted to come upon deck. It ferves to keep the different fexes apart; and as there are fmall holes in it, wherein blunderbuffes are fixed, and fometimes a cannon, it is found very convenient for quelling the infurrections that now and then happen. Another door is made in the lattice or net-work at the ladder, by which you enter the ship. This door is guarded by a centinal during the day, and is locked at night. At the head of the ship there is a third door, for the ufe of the failors, which is fecured in the fame manner as that at the gangway. There is alfo in the roof a large trap-door, through which the goods intended for barter, the water cafks, &c. are hoifted out or in.

The defign of this houfe is to fecure thofe on board from the heat of the fun, which in this latitude is intenfe, and from the wind and rain, which at particular feafons, are likewife extremely violent. It anfwers thefe purpofes however but very ineffectually. The flight texture of the mats admits both the wind and the rain, whenever it hap-

pens

pens to be violent, though at the same time, it increases the heat of the ship to a very pernicious degree, especially between decks. The increased warmth occasioned by this means, together with the smoke produced from the green mangrove, (the usual firewood) which, for want of a current of air to carry it off, collects itself in large quantities, and infests every part of the ship, render a vessel during its stay here very unhealthy. The smoke also, by its acrimonious quality, often produces inflammations in the eyes, which terminates sometimes in the loss of sight.

Another purpose for which these temporary houses are erected, is, in order to prevent the purchased negroes from leaping overboard. This, the horrors of their situation frequently impel them to attempt; and they now and then effect it, notwithstanding all the precautions that are taken, by forcing their way through the lattice work.

The slave ships generally lie near a mile below the town, in Bonny River, in seven or eight fathom water. Sometimes fifteen sail, English and French, but chiefly the former, meet here together. Soon after they cast anchor, the captains go on shore, to make known their arrival, and to inquire into the state of the trade. They likewise invite the kings of Bonny to come on board, to whom, previous to breaking bulk, they usually make presents (in that country termed *dashes*) which generally consist of pieces of cloth, cotton, chintz, silk handkerchiefs, and other India goods, and sometimes of brandy, wine, or beer.

When I was at Bonny a few years ago, it was the residence of two kings, whose names were *Norfolk* and *Peppel*. The houses of these princes were not distinguished from the cottages or huts of which the town consists, in any other manner,

A 4   than

than by being of somewhat larger dimensions, and surrounded with warehouses containing European goods, designed for the purchase of slaves. These slaves, which the kings procure in the same manner as the black traders do theirs, are sold by them to the ships. And for every negroe sold there by the traders, the kings receive a duty, which amounts to a considerable sum in the course of a year. This duty is collected by officers, stationed on board the ships, who are termed *officer boys*; a denomination which it is thought they received from the English.

The kings of Bonny are absolute, though elective. They are assisted in the government by a small number of persons of a certain rank, who stile themselves *parliament gentlemen*; an office which they generally hold for life. Every ship, on its arrival, is expected to send a present to these gentlemen, of a small quantity of bread and beef, and likewise to treat them as often as they come on board. When they do this, their approach to the ship is announced by blowing through a hollow elephant's tooth, which produces a sound resembling that of a post-horn.

After the kings have been on board, and have received the usual presents, permission is granted by them for trafficking with any of the black traders. When the royal guests return from the ships, they are saluted by the guns.

From the time of the arrival of the ships to their departure, which is usually near three months, scarce a day passes without some negroes being purchased, and carried on board; sometimes in small, and sometimes in larger numbers. The whole number taken on board, depends, in a great measure, on circumstances. In a voyage I once made, our stock of merchandize was exhausted in
the

the purchase of about 380 negroes, which was expected to have procured 500. The number of English and French ships then at Bonny, had so far raised the price of negroes, as to occasion this difference.

The reverse (and a *happy* reverse I think I may call it) was known during the late war. When I was last at Bonny, I frequently made inquiries on this head, of one of the black traders, whose intelligence I believe I can depend upon. He informed me that only one ship had been there for three years during that period; and that was the *Moseley-Hill*, Captain Ewing, from Leverpool, who made an extraordinary purchase, as he found negroes remarkably cheap from the dulness of trade. Upon further inquiring of my black acquaintance, what was the consequence of this decay of their trade, he shrugged up his shoulders, and answered, *only making us traders poorer, and obliging us to work for our maintenance.* One of these black merchants being informed, that a particular set of people, called Quakers, were for abolishing the trade, he said, *it was a very bad thing, as they should then be reduced to the same state they were in during the war, when, through poverty, they were obliged to dig the ground and plant yams.*

I was once upon the coast of Angola also, when there had not been a slave ship at the river Ambris for five years previous to our arrival, although a place to which many usually resort every year; and the failure of the trade for that perod, as far as we could learn, had not any other effect, than to restore peace and confidence among the natives; which, upon the arrival of any ships, is immediately destroyed, by the inducement then held forth in the purchase of slaves. And during the suspension of trade at Bonny, as above-mentioned, none of the dreadful proceedings, which are

so

fo confidently aſſerted to be the natural conſe-
quence of it, were known. The reduction of the
price of negroes, and the poverty of the black
traders, appear to have been the only *bad* effects of
the diſcontinuance of trade; the *good* ones were, *moſt
probably*, the reſtoration of peace and confidence a-
mong the natives, and a ſuſpenſion of kidnapping.

When the ſhips have diſpoſed of all their merchandize in the purchaſe of negroes, and have
laid in their ſtock of wood, water, and yams, they
prepare for ſailing, by getting up the yards and
topmaſts, reeving the running rigging, bending
the ſails, and by taking down the temporary houſe.
They then drop down the river, to wait for a
favourable opportunity to paſs over the bar,
which is formed by a number of ſand-banks lying
acroſs the mouth of the river, with navigable chan-
nels between them. It is not uncommon for ſhips
to get upon the bar, and ſometimes they are loſt.

The firſt place the ſlave ſhips touch at in their
paſſage to the Weſt-Indies, is either the Iſland of
St. Thomas, or Princes Iſland, where they uſually
carry their ſick on ſhore, for the benefit of the air,
and likewiſe repleniſh their ſtock of water. The
former of theſe iſlands is nearly circular, being one
hundred and twenty miles round, and lies exactly
under the equator, about forty-five leagues from
the African continent. It abounds with wood and
water, and produces Indian corn, rice, fruits, ſugar, and ſome cinnamon. The air is rather prejudicial to an European conſtitution, neverthelefs
it is well peopled by the Portugueſe. Princes
Iſland, which is much ſmaller, lies in 1 deg. 30
min. north latitude, and likewiſe produces Indian corn, and a variety of fruits and roots, beſides
ſugar canes. Black cattle, hogs, and goats are
numerous there; but it is infeſted with a miſ-
chievous and dangerous ſpecies of monkeys.

During

During one of the voyages I made, I was landed upon the Island of St. Thomas, with near one hundred sick negroes, who were placed in an old house, taken on purpose for their reception. Little benefit however accrued from their going on shore, as several of them died there, and the remainder continued nearly in the same situation as when they were landed, though our continuance was prolonged for about twelve days, and the island is deemed upon the whole healthy.

Upon the arrival of the slave ships in the West-Indies, a day is soon fixed for the sale of their cargoes. And this is done by different modes, and often by one they term a *scramble,* of which some account will be given, when the sale of the negroes is treated of.

The whole of their cargoes being disposed of, the ships are immediately made ready to proceed to sea. It is very seldom, however, that they are not detained, for want of a sufficient number of sailors to navigate the ship, as this trade may justly be denominated the grave of seamen. Though the crews of the ships upon their leaving England, generally amount to between forty and fifty men, scarcely three-fourths, and sometimes not one-third of the complement, ever return to the port from whence they sailed, through mortality and desertion ; the causes of which I shall speak of under another head.

The time during which the slave ships are absent from England, varies according to the destination of the voyage, and the number of ships they happen to meet on the coast. To Bonny, or Old and New Calabar, a voyage is usually performed in about ten months. Those to the Windward and Gold Coasts, are rather more uncertain, but in general from fifteen to eighteen months.

The

The Manner in which the Slaves are procured.

After permission has been obtained for *breaking trade*, as it is termed, the captains go ashore, from time to time, to examine the negroes that are exposed to sale, and to make their purchases. The unhappy wretches thus disposed of, are bought by the black traders at fairs, which are held for that purpose, at the distance of upwards of two hundred miles from the sea coast; and these fairs are said to be supplied from an interior part of the country. Many negroes, upon being questioned relative to the places of their nativity have asserted, that they have travelled during the revolution of several moons, (their usual method of calculating time) before they have reached the places where they were purchased by the black traders. At these fairs, which are held at uncertain periods, but generally every six weeks, several thousands are frequently exposed to sale, who had been collected from all parts of the country for a very considerable distance round. While I was upon the coast, during one of the voyages I made, the black traders brought down, in different canoes, from twelve to fifteen hundred negroes, which had been purchased at one fair. They consisted chiefly of men and boys, the women seldom exceeding a third of the whole number. From forty to two hundred negroes are generally purchased at a time by the black traders, according to the opulence of the buyer; and consist confift of thofe of all ages, from a month, to fixty years and upwards. Scarce any age or fituation is deemed an exception, the price being proportionable. Women fometimes form a part of them, who happen to be fo far advanced in their pregnancy, as to be delivered during their journey from the fairs to the coaft; and I have frequently feen inftances of deliveries on board fhip. The flaves purchafed at thefe fairs are only for the fupply of the markets at Bonny, and Old and New Calabar.

There is great reafon to believe, that moft of the negroes fhipped off from the coaft of Africa, are *kidnapped*. But the extreme care taken by the black traders to prevent the Europeans from gaining any intelligence of their modes of proceeding; the great diftance inland from whence the negroes are brought; and our ignorance of their language, (with which, very frequently, the black traders themfelves are equally unacquainted) prevent our obtaining fuch information on this head as we could wifh. I have, however, by means of occafional inquiries, made through interpreters, procured fome intelligence relative to the point, and fuch, as I think, puts the matter beyond a doubt.

From thefe I fhall feleƈt the following ftriking inftances :—While I was in employ on board one of the flave fhips, a negroe informed me, that being one evening invited to drink with fome of the black traders, upon his going away, they attempted to feize him. As he was very aƈtive, he evaded their defign, and got out of their hands. He was however prevented from effeƈting his efcape by a large dog, which laid hold of him, and compelled him to fubmit. Thefe creatures are kept by many of the traders for that purpofe;
and

and being trained to the inhuman sport, they appear to be much pleased with it.

I was likewise told by a negroe woman, that as she was on her return home, one evening, from some neighbours, to whom she had been making a visit by invitation, she was kidnapped; and, notwithstanding she was big with child, sold for a slave. This transaction happened a considerable way up the country, and she had passed through the hands of several purchasers before she reached the ship. A man and his son, according to their own information, were seized by professed kidnappers, while they were planting yams, and sold for slaves. This likewise happened in the interior parts of the country, and after passing through several hands, they were purchased for the ship to which I belonged.

It frequently happens, that those who kidnap others, are themselves, in their turns, seized and sold. A negroe in the West-Indies informed me, that after having been employed in kidnapping others, he had experienced this reverse. And he assured me, that it was a common incident among his countrymen.

Continual enmity is thus fostered among the negroes of Africa, and all social intercourse between them destroyed; which most assuredly would not be the case, had they not these opportunities of finding a ready sale for each other.

During my stay on the coast of Africa, I was an eye-witness of the following transaction :—— A black trader invited a negroe, who resided a little way up the country, to come and see him. After the entertainment was over, the trader proposed to his guest, to treat him with a sight of one of the ships lying in the river. The unsuspicious countryman readily consented, and accompanied

companied the trader in a canoe to the side of
the ship, which he viewed with pleasure and asto-
nishment. While he was thus employed, some
black traders on board, who appeared to be in
the secret, leaped into the canoe, seized the un-
fortunate man, and dragging him into the ship,
immediately sold him.

Previous to my being in this employ, I enter-
tained a belief, as many others have done, that
the kings and principal men *breed* negroes for
sale, as we do cattle. During the different times
I was in the country, I took no little pains to
satisfy myself in this particular ; but notwithstanding I made many inquiries, I was not able
to obtain the least intelligence of this being the
case, which it is more than probable I should
have done, had such a practice prevailed. All
the information I could procure, confirms me in
the belief, that to *kidnapping*, and to crimes, (and
many of these fabricated as a pretext) the slave
trade owes its chief support.

The following instance tends to prove, that the
last mentioned artifice is often made use of. Several
black traders, one of whom was a person of consequence, and exercised an authority somewhat similar
to that of our magistrates, being in want of some
particular kind of merchandize, and not having
a slave to barter for it, they accused a fisherman,
at the river Ambris, with extortion in the sale of
his fish ; and as they were interested in the deci-
sion, they immediately adjudged the poor fellow
guilty, and condemned him to be sold. He was
accordingly purchased by the ship to which I belonged, and brought on board.

As an additional proof that kidnapping is not
only the general, but almost the sole mode, by
which slaves are procured, the black traders, in
purchasing

purchasing them, chuse those which are the rough-
est and most hardy; alleging, that the smooth
negroes have been *gentlemen*. By this observation
we may conclude they mean that nothing but
fraud or force could have reduced these smooth-
skinned gentlemen to a state of slavery.

It may not be here unworthy of remark, in order to prove that the wars among the Africans do
not furnish the number of slaves they are supposed
to do, that I never saw any negroes with recent
wounds; which must have been the consequence, at
least with some of them, had they been taken in
battle. And it being the particular province of
the surgeon to examine the slaves when they are
purchased, such a circumstance could not have
escaped my observation. As a farther corrobo-
ration, it might be remarked, that on the Gold
and Windward Coasts, where fairs are not held,
the number of slaves procured at a time are
usually very small.

The preparations made at Bonny by the black
traders, upon setting out for the fairs which are
held up the country, are very considerable. From
twenty to thirty canoes, capable of containing
thirty or forty negroes each, are assembled for this
purpose; and such goods put on board them as
they expect will be wanted for the purchase of the
number of slaves they intend to buy. When their
loading is completed, they commence their voyage, with colours flying and musick playing; and
in about ten or eleven days, they generally return
to Bonny with full cargoes. As soon as the canoes arrive at the trader's landing-place, the purchased negroes are cleaned, and oiled with palm
oil; and on the following day they are exposed
for sale to the captains.

The

The black traders do not always purchase their slaves at the same rate. The speed with which the information of the arrival of ships upon the coast is conveyed to the fairs, considering it is the interest of the traders to keep them ignorant, is really surprising. In a very short time after any ships arrive upon the coast, especially if several make their appearance together, those who dispose of the negroes at the fairs are frequently known to increase the price of them.

These fairs are not the only means, though they are the chief, by which the black traders on the coast are supplied with negroes. Small parties of them, from five to ten, are frequently brought to the houses of the traders, by those who make a practice of kidnapping; and who are constantly employed in procuring a supply, while purchasers are to be found.

When the negroes, whom the black traders have to dispose of, are shewn to the European purchasers, they first examine them relative to their age. They then minutely inspect their persons, and inquire into the state of their health; if they are afflicted with any infirmity, or are deformed, or have bad eyes or teeth; if they are lame, or weak in the joints, or distorted in the back, or of a slender make, or are narrow in the chest; in short, if they have been, or are afflicted in any manner, so as to render them incapable of much labour; if any of the foregoing defects are discovered in them, they are rejected. But if approved of, they are generally taken on board the ship the same evening. The purchaser has liberty to return on the following morning, but not afterwards, such as upon re-examination are found exceptionable.

B   The

The traders frequently beat thofe negroes which are objected to by the captains, and ufe them with great feverity. It matters not whether they are refufed on account of age, illnefs, deformity, or for any other reafon. At New Calabar, in particular, the traders have frequently been known to put them to death. Inftances have happened at that place, that the traders, when any of their negroes have been objected to, have dropped their canoes under the ftern of the veffel, and inftantly beheaded them, in fight of the captain.

Upon the Windward Coaft, another mode of procuring flaves is purfued; which is, by what they term *boating*; a mode that is very pernicious and deftructive to the crews of the fhips. The failors, who are employed upon this trade, go in boats up the rivers, feeking for negroes, among the villages fituated on the banks of them. But this method is very flow, and not always effectual. For, after being abfent from the fhip during a fortnight or three weeks, they fometimes return with only from eight to twelve negroes. Numbers of thefe are procured in confequence of alleged crimes, which, as before obferved, whenever any fhips are upon the coaft, are more productive than at any other period. Kidnapping, however, prevails here.

I have good reafon to believe, that of one hundred and twenty negroes, which were purchafed for the fhip to which I then belonged, then lying at the river Ambris, by far the greater part, if not the whole, were kidnapped. This, with various other inftances, confirms me in the belief that kidnapping is the fund which fupplies the thoufands of negroes annually fold off thefe extenfive Windward, and other Coafts, where boating prevails.

Treatment

Treatment of the Slaves.

As soon as the wretched Africans, purchased at the fairs, fall into the hands of the black traders, they experience an earnest of those dreadful sufferings which they are doomed in future to undergo. And there is not the least room to doubt, but that even before they can reach the fairs, great numbers perish from cruel usage, want of food, travelling through inhospitable deserts, &c. They are brought from the places where they are purchased to Bonny, &c. in canoes; at the bottom of which they lie, having their hands tied with a kind of willow twigs, and a strict watch is kept over them. Their usage in other respects, during the time of the passage, which generally lasts several days, is equally cruel. Their allowance of food is so scanty, that it is barely sufficient to support nature. They are, besides, much exposed to the violent rains which frequently fall here, being covered only with mats that afford but a slight defence; and as there is usually water at the bottom of the canoes, from their leaking, they are scarcely ever dry.

Nor do these unhappy beings, after they become the property of the Europeans (from whom, as a more civilized people, more humanity might naturally be expected) find their situation in the least amended. Their treatment is no less rigorous. The men negroes, on being brought aboard the ship, are immediately fastened together, two and two, by hand-cuffs on their wrists, and by irons rivetted on their legs. They are then sent down between the decks, and placed in an apartment partitioned off for that purpose. The wo-

men

men likewife are placed in a feparate apartment between decks, but without being ironed. And an adjoining room, on the fame deck, is befides appointed for the boys. Thus are they all placed in different apartments.

But at the fame time, they are frequently ftowed fo clofe, as to admit of no other pofture than lying on their fides. Neither will the height between decks, unlefs directly under the grating, permit them the indulgence of an erect pofture; efpecially where there are platforms, which is generally the cafe. Thefe platforms are a kind of fhelf, about eight or nine feet in breadth, extending from the fide of the fhip towards the centre. They are placed nearly midway between the decks, at the diftance of two or three feet from each deck. Upon thefe the negroes are ftowed in the fame manner as they are on the deck underneath.

In each of the apartments are placed three or four large buckets, of a conical form, being near two feet in diameter at the bottom, and only one foot at the top, and in depth about twenty-eight inches; to which, when neceffary, the negroes have recourfe. It often happens, that thofe who are placed at a diftance from the buckets, in endeavouring to get to them, tumble over their companions, in confequence of their being fhackled. Thefe accidents, although unavoidable, are productive of continual quarrels, in which fome of them are always bruifed. In this diftreffed fituation, unable to proceed, and prevented from getting to the tubs, they defift from the attempt; and, as the neceffities of nature are not to be repelled, eafe themfelves as they lie. This becomes a frefh fource of broils and difturbances, and tends to render the condition of the poor cap-
tive

tive wretches ftill more uncomfortable. The nuiſance ariſing from theſe circumſtances, is not unfrequently increaſed by the tubs being much too ſmall for the purpoſe intended, and their being uſually emptied but once every day. The rule for doing this, however, varies in different ſhips, according to the attention paid to the health and convenience of the ſlaves by the captain.

About eight o'clock in the morning the negroes are generally brought upon deck. Their irons being examined, a long chain, which is locked to a ring-bolt, fixed in the deck, is run through the rings of the ſhackles of the men, and then locked to another ring-bolt, fixed alſo in the deck. By this means fifty or ſixty, and ſometimes more, are faſtened to one chain, in order to prevent them from riſing, or endeavouring to eſcape. If the weather proves favourable, they are permitted to remain in that ſituation till four or five in the afternoon, when they are diſengaged from the chain, and ſent down.

The diet of the negroes, while on board, conſiſts chiefly of horſe-beans, boiled to the conſiſtence of a pulp; of boiled yams and rice, and ſometimes of a ſmall quantity of beef or pork. The latter are frequently taken from the proviſions laid in for the ſailors. They ſometimes make uſe of a ſauce, compoſed of palm-oil, mixed with flour, water, and pepper, which the ſailors call *ſlabber-ſauce*. Yams are the favourite food of the Eboe, or Bight negroes, and rice or corn, of thoſe from the Gold and Windward Coaſts; each preferring the produce of their native ſoil.

In their own country, the negroes in general live on animal food and fiſh, with roots, yams, and Indian corn. The horſe-beans and rice, with

B 3 which

which they are fed aboard ship, are chiefly taken from Europe. The latter, indeed, is sometimes purchased on the coast, being far superior to any other.

The Gold Coast negroes scarcely ever refuse any food that is offered them, and they generally eat larger quantities of whatever is placed before them, than any other species of negroes, whom they likewise excel in strength of body and mind. Most of the slaves have such an aversion to the horse-beans, that unless they are narrowly watched, when fed upon deck, they will throw them overboard, or in each other's faces when they quarrel.

They are commonly fed twice a day, about eight o'clock in the morning and four in the afternoon. In most ships they are only fed with their *own food* once a day. Their food is served up to them in tubs, about the size of a small water bucket. They are placed round these tubs in companies of ten to each tub, out of which they feed themselves with wooden spoons. These they soon lose, and when they are not allowed others, they feed themselves with their hands. In favourable weather they are fed upon deck, but in bad weather their food is given them below. Numberless quarrels take place among them during their meals; more especially when they are put upon short allowance, which frequently happens, if the passage from the coast of Guinea to the West-India islands, proves of unusual length. In that case, the weak are obliged to be content with a very scanty portion. Their allowance of water is about half a pint each at every meal. It is handed round in a bucket, and given to each negroe in a pannekin; a small utensil with a strait handle, somewhat similar to a sauce-boat. However, when the ships fhips approach the iflands with a favourable breeze, they are no longer reftricted.

Upon the negroes refufing to take fuftenance, I have feen coals of fire, glowing hot, put on a fhovel, and placed fo near their lips, as to fcorch and burn them. And this has been accompanied with threats, of forcing them to fwallow the coals, if they any longer perfifted in refufing to eat. Thefe means have generally had the defired effect. I have alfo been credibly informed, that a certain captain in the flave trade, poured melted lead on fuch of the negroes as obftinately refufed their food.

Exercife being deemed neceffary for the prefer-vation of their health, they are fometimes obliged to dance, when the weather will permit their com-ing on deck. If they go about it reluctantly, or do not move with agility, they are flogged; a perfon ftanding by them all the time with a cat-o'-nine-tails in his hand for that purpofe. Their mufick, upon thefe occafions, confifts of a drum, fometimes with only one head; and when that is worn out, they do not fcruple to make ufe of the bottom of one of the tubs before defcribed. The poor wretches are frequently compelled to fing alfo; but when they do fo, their fongs are gene-rally, as may naturally be expected, melancholy lamentations of their exile from their native country.

The women are furnifhed with beads for the purpofe of affording them fome diverfion. But this end is generally defeated by the fquabbles which are occafioned, in confequence of their ftealing them from each other.

On board fome fhips, the common failors are allowed to have intercourfe with fuch of the black women whofe confent they can procure. And fome

of

of them have been known to take the inconstancy of their paramours so much to heart, as to leap overboard and drown themselves. The officers are permitted to indulge their passions among them at pleasure, and sometimes are guilty of such brutal excesses, as disgrace human nature.

The hardships and inconveniencies suffered by the negroes during the passage, are scarcely to be enumerated or conceived. They are far more violently affected by the sea-sickness, than the Europeans. It frequently terminates in death, especially among the women. But the exclusion of the fresh air is among the most intolerable. For the purpose of admitting this needful refreshment, most of the ships in the slave-trade are provided, between the decks, with five or six air-ports on each side of the ship, of about six inches in length, and four in breadth; in addition to which, some few ships, but not one in twenty, have what they denominate *wind-sails*. But whenever the sea is rough, and the rain heavy, it becomes necessary to shut these, and every other conveyance by which the air is admitted. The fresh air being thus excluded, the negroes rooms very soon grow intolerably hot. The confined air, rendered noxious by the effluvia exhaled from their bodies, and by being repeatedly breathed, soon produces fevers and fluxes, which generally carries off great numbers of them.

During the voyages I made, I was frequently a witness to the fatal effects of this exclusion of the fresh air. I will give one instance, as it serves to convey some idea, though a very faint one, of the sufferings of those unhappy beings whom we wantonly drag from their native country, and doom to perpetual labour and captivity. Some wet and blowing weather having occasioned the port-holes

to

to be shut, and the grating to be covered, fluxes and fevers among the negroes ensued. While they were in this situation, my profession requiring it, I frequently went down among them, till at length their apartments became so extremely hot, as to be only sufferable for a very short time. But the excessive heat was not the only thing that rendered their situation intolerable. The deck, that is, the floor of their rooms, was so covered with the blood and mucus which had proceeded from them in consequence of the flux, that it resembled a slaughter-house. It is not in the power of the human imagination, to picture to itself a situation more dreadful or disgusting. Numbers of the slaves having fainted, they were carried upon deck, where several of them died, and the rest were, with great difficulty, restored. It had nearly proved fatal to me also. The climate was too warm to admit the wearing of any clothing but a shirt, and that I had pulled off before I went down; notwithstanding which, by only continuing among them for about a quarter of an hour, I was so overcome with the heat, stench, and foul air, that I had nearly fainted; and it was not without assistance, that I could get upon deck. The consequence was, that I soon after fell sick of the same disorder, from which I did not recover for several months.

A circumstance of this kind, sometimes repeatedly happens in the course of a voyage; and often to a greater degree than what has just been described; particularly when the slaves are much crowded, which was not the case at that time, the ship having more than a hundred short of the number she was to have taken in.

This devastation, great as it was, some few years ago was greatly exceeded on board a Liverpool ship.

I shall

I fhall particularize the circumftances of it, as a more glaring inftance of an infatiable thirft for gain, or of lefs attention to the lives and happinefs even of that defpifed and oppreffed race of mortals, the fable inhabitants of Africa, perhaps was never exceeded; though indeed feveral fimilar inftances have been known.

This fhip, though a much fmaller fhip than that in which the event I have juft mentioned happened, took on board at Bonny, at leaft fix hundred negroes; but according to the information of the black traders, from whom I received the intelligence immediately after the fhip failed, they amounted to near *feven hundred*. By purchafing fo great a number, the flaves were fo crowded, that they were even obliged to lie one upon another. This occafioned fuch a mortality among them, that, without meeting with unufual bad weather, or having a longer voyage than common, nearly one half of them died before the fhip arrived in the Weft-Indies.

That the publick may be able to form fome idea of the almoft incredible fmall fpace into which fo large a number of negroes were crammed, the following particulars of this fhip are given. According to Leverpool cuftom fhe meafured 235 tons. Her width acrofs the beam, 25 feet. Length between the decks, 92 feet, which was divided into four rooms, thus:

Store room, in which there were not any negroes placed } 15 feet

Negroes rooms — mens room — about 45 feet
womens ditto about 10 feet
boys ditto about 22 feet

Total room for negroes 77 feet

Exclusive of the platform before described, from 8 to 9 feet in breadth, and equal in length to that of the rooms.

It may be worthy of remark, that the ships in this trade, are usually fitted out to receive only one third women negroes, or perhaps a smaller number, which the dimensions of the room allotted for them, above given, plainly shew, but in a greater disproportion.

One would naturally suppose, that an attention to their own interest, would prompt the owners of the Guinea ships not to suffer the captains to take on board a greater number of negroes than the ship would allow room sufficient for them to lie with ease to themselves, or, at least, without rubbing against each other. However that may be, a more striking instance than the above, of avarice, completely and deservedly disappointed, was surely never displayed; for there is little room to doubt, but that in consequence of the expected premium usually allowed to the captains, of 6l. per cent. sterling on the produce of the negroes, this vessel was so thronged as to occasion such a heavy loss.

The place allotted for the sick negroes is under the half deck, where they lie on the bare planks.

planks. By this means, those who are emaciated, frequently have their skin, and even their flesh, entirely rubbed off, by the motion of the ship, from the prominent parts of the shoulders, elbows, and hips, so as to render the bones in those parts quite bare. And some of them, by constantly lying in the blood and mucus, that had flowed from those afflicted with the flux, and which, as before observed, is generally so violent as to prevent their being kept clean, have their flesh much sooner rubbed off, than those who have only to contend with the mere friction of the ship. The excruciating pain which the poor sufferers feel from being obliged to continue in such a dreadful situation, frequently for several weeks, in case they happen to live so long, is not to be conceived or described. Few, indeed, are ever able to withstand the fatal effects of it. The utmost skill of the surgeon is here ineffectual. If plaisters be applied, they are very soon displaced by the friction of the ship; and when bandages are used, the negroes very soon take them off, and appropriate them to other purposes.

The surgeon, upon going between decks, in the morning, to examine the situation of the slaves, frequently finds several dead; and among the men, sometimes a dead and living negroe fastened by their irons together. When this is the case, they are brought upon the deck, and being laid on the grating, the living negroe is disengaged, and the dead one thrown overboard.

It may not be improper here to remark, that the surgeons employed in the Guinea trade, are generally driven to engage in so disagreeable an employ by the confined state of their finances. An exertion of the greatest skill and attention could afford the diseased negroes little relief, so long as the causes of their diseases, namely, the

breathing

breathing of a putrid atmosphere, and wallowing in their own excrements, remain. When once the fever and dysentery get to any height at sea, a cure is scarcely ever effected.

Almost the only means by which the surgeon can render himself useful to the slaves, is, by seeing that their food is properly cooked, and distributed among them. It is true, when they arrive near the markets for which they are destined, care is taken to polish them for sale, by an application of the lunar caustic to such as are afflicted with the yaws. This, however, affords but a temporary relief, as the disease most assuredly breaks out, whenever the patient is put upon a vegetable diet.

It has been asserted, in favour of the captains in this trade, that the sick slaves are usually fed from their tables. The great number generally ill at a time, proves the falsity of such an assertion. Were even a captain *disposed* to do this, how could he feed half the slaves in the ship from his own table? for it is well known, that *more than half* are often sick at a time. Two or three perhaps may be fed.

The loss of slaves, through mortality, arising from the causes just mentioned, are frequently very considerable. In the voyage lately referred to (not the Leverpool ship before-mentioned) one hundred and five, out of three hundred and eighty, died in the passage. A proportion seemingly very great, but by no means uncommon. One half, sometimes two thirds, and even beyond that, have been known to perish. Before we left Bonny River, no less than fifteen died of fevers and dysenteries, occasioned by their confinement. On the Windward Coast, where slaves are procured more slowly, very few die, in proportion to the numbers which die at

Bonny,

Bonny, and at Old and New Calabar, where they are obtained much faster; the latter being of a more delicate make and habit.

The havock made among the seamen engaged in this destructive commerce, will be noticed in another part; and will be found to make no inconsiderable addition to the unnecessary waste of life just represented.

As very few of the negroes can so far brook the loss of their liberty, and the hardships they endure, as to bear them with any degree of patience, they are ever upon the watch to take advantage of the least negligence in their oppressors. Insurrections are frequently the consequence; which are seldom suppressed without much bloodshed. Sometimes these are successful, and the whole ship's company is cut off. They are likewise always ready to seize every opportunity for committing some act of desperation to free themselves from their miserable state; and notwithstanding the restraints under which they are laid, they often succeed.

While a ship, to which I belonged, lay in Bonny River, one evening, a short time before our departure, a lot of negroes, consisting of about ten, was brought on board; when one of them, in a favourable moment, forced his way through the net-work on the larboard side of the vessel, jumped overboard, and was supposed to have been devoured by the sharks.

During the time we were there, fifteen negroes belonging to a vessel from Liverpool, found means to throw themselves into the river; very few were saved; and the residue fell a sacrifice to the sharks. A similar instance took place in a French ship while we lay there.

Circumstances of this kind are very frequent.

On

On the coaft of Angola, at the River Ambris, the following incident happened :——During the time of our reſiding on ſhore, we erected a tent to ſhelter ourſelves from the weather. After having been there ſeveral weeks, and being unable to purchaſe the number of ſlaves we wanted, through the oppoſition of another Engliſh ſlave veſſel, we determined to leave the place. The night before our departure, the tent was ſtruck; which was no ſooner perceived by ſome of the negroe women on board, than it was conſidered as a prelude to our ſailing; and about eighteen of them, when they were ſent between decks, threw themſelves into the ſea through one of the gun ports; the ſhip carrying guns between decks. They weie all of them, however, excepting one, ſoon picked up; and that which was miſſing, was, not long after, taken about a mile from the ſhore.

I once knew a negroe woman, too ſenſible of her woes, who pined for a conſiderable time, and was taken ill of a fever and dyſentery; when declaring it to be her determination to die, ſhe refuſed all food and medical aid, and, in about a fortnight after, expired. On being thrown overboard, her body was inſtantly torn to pieces by the ſharks.

The following circumſtance alſo came within my knowledge. A young female negroe, falling into a deſponding way, it was judged neceſſary, in order to attempt her recovery, to ſend her on ſhore, to the hut of one of the black traders. Elevated with the proſpect of regaining her liberty by this unexpected ſtep, ſhe ſoon recovered her uſual chearfulneſs; but hearing, by accident, that it was intended to take her on board the ſhip again, the poor young creature hung herſelf.

It

It frequently happens that the negroes, on being purchaſed by the Europeans, become raving mad; and many of them die in that ſtate; particularly the women. While I was one day aſhore at Bonny, I ſaw a middle aged ſtout woman, who had been brought down from a fair the preceding day, chained to the poſt of a black trader's door, in a ſtate of furious inſanity. On board a ſhip in Bonny River, I ſaw a young negroe woman chained to the deck, who had loſt her ſenſes, ſoon after ſhe was purchaſed and taken on board. In a former voyage, on board a ſhip to which I belonged, we were obliged to confine a female negroe, of about twenty-three years of age, on her becoming a lunatic. She was afterwards ſold during one of her lucid intervals.

One morning, upon examining the place allotted for the ſick negroes, I perceived that one of them, who was ſo emaciated as ſcarcely to be able to walk, was miſſing, and was convinced that he muſt have gone overboard in the night, probably to put a more expeditious period to his ſufferings. And, to conclude on this ſubject, I could not help being ſenſibly affected, on a former voyage, at obſerving with what apparent eagerneſs a black woman ſeized ſome dirt from off an African yam, and put it into her mouth; ſeeming to rejoice at the opportunity of poſſeſſing ſome of her native earth.

From theſe inſtances I think it may be clearly deduced, that the unhappy Africans are not bereſt of the finer feelings, but have a ſtrong attachment to their native country, together with a juſt ſenſe of the value of liberty. And the ſituation of the miſerable beings above deſcribed, more forcibly urge the neceſſity of aboliſhing a trade which is the ſource of ſuch evils, than the moſt eloquent harangue, or perſuaſive arguments could do.

Sale

Sale of the Slaves.

When the ships arrive in the West-Indies, (the chief mart for this inhuman merchandize), the slaves are disposed of, as I have before observed, by different methods. Sometimes the mode of disposal, is that of selling them by what is termed a *scramble*; and a day is soon fixed for that purpose. But previous thereto, the sick, or refuse slaves, of which there are frequently many, are usually conveyed on shore,, and sold at a tavern by vendue, or public auction. These, in general, are purchased by the Jews and surgeons, but chiefly the former, upon speculation, at so low a price as five or six dollars a head. I was informed by a mulatto woman, that she purchased a sick slave at Grenada, upon speculation, for the small sum of one dollar, as the poor wretch was apparently dying of the flux. It seldom happens that any, who are carried ashore in the emaciated state to which they are generally reduced by that disorder, long survive their landing. I once saw sixteen conveyed on shore, and sold in the foregoing manner, the whole of whom died before I left the island, which was within a short time after. Sometimes the captains march their slaves through the town at which they intend to dispose of them; and then place them in rows where they are examined and purchased.

The mode of selling them by scramble having fallen under my observation the oftenest, I shal be more particular in describing it. Being some years ago, at one of the islands in the West-In-

dies,

dies, I was witnefs to a fale by fcramble, where
about 250 negroes were fold. Upor. this occafion
all the negroes fcrambled for bear an equal price;
which is agreed upon between the captains and
the purchafers before the fale begins.

On a day appointed, the negroes were landed,
and placed altogether in a large yard, belonging
to the merchants to whom the fhip was configned.
As foon as the hour agreed on arrived, the doors
of the yard were fuddenly thrown open, and in
rufhed a confiderable number of purchafers, with
all the ferocity of brutes. Some inftantly feized
fuch of the negroes as they could conveniently lay
hold of with their hands. Others, being prepared
with feveral handkerchiefs tied together, encircled
with thefe as many as they were able. While
others, by means of a rope, effected the fame purpofe. It is fcarcely poffible to defcribe the con-
fufion of which this mode of felling is productive.
It likewife caufes much animofity among the purchafers, who, not unfrequently upon thefe occafions, fall out and quarrel with each other. The
poor aftonifhed negroes were fo much terrified by
thefe proceedings, that feveral of them, through
fear, climbed over the walls of the court yard,
and ran wild about the town; but were foon
hunted down and retaken.

While on a former voyage from Africa to
Kingfton in Jamaica, I faw a fale there by fcramble, on board a fnow. The negroes were collected together upon the main and quarter
decks, and the fhip was darkened by fails fuf-
pended over them, in order to prevent the purchafers from being able to fee, fo as to pick or
chufe. The fignal being given, the buyers rufhed
in, as ufual, to feize their prey; when the negroes appeared to be extremely terrified, and near
thirty

thirty of them jumped into the fea. But they were all foon retaken, chiefly by boats from other ſhips.

On board a ſhip, lying at Port Maria, in Jamaica, I ſaw another ſcramble; in which, as uſual, the poor negroes were greatly terrified. The women, in particular, clang to each other in agonies ſcarcely to be conceived, ſhrieking through exceſs of terror, at the ſavage manner in which their brutal purchaſers ruſhed upon, and ſeized them. Though humanity, one ſhould imagine, would dictate the captains to apprize the poor negroes of the mode by which they were to be ſold, and by that means to guard them, in ſome degree, againſt the ſurprize and terror which muſt attend it, I never knew that any notice of the ſcramble was given to them. Nor have I any reaſon to think that it is done; or that this mode of ſale is leſs frequent at this time, than formerly.

Various are the deceptions made uſe of in the diſpoſal of the ſick ſlaves; and many of theſe, ſuch as muſt excite in every humane mind, the livelieſt ſenſations of horror. I have been well informed, that a Liverpool captain boaſted of his having cheated ſome Jews by the following ſtratagem: A lot of ſlaves, afflicted with the flux, being about to be landed for ſale, he directed the ſurgeon to ſtop the anus of each of them with oakum. Thus prepared, they were landed, and taken to the accuſtomed place of ſale; where, being unable to ſtand but for a very ſhort time, they are uſually permitted to ſit. The Jews, when they examine them, oblige them to ſtand up, in order to ſee if there be any diſcharge; and when they do not perceive this appearance, they conſider it as a ſymptom of recovery.

C 2 In

In the prefent inftance, fuch an appearance being
prevented, the bargain was ftruck, and they were
accordingly fold. But it was not long before a
difcovery enfued. The excruciating pain which
the prevention of a difcharge of fuch an acrimonious nature occafioned, not being to be borne
by the poor wretches, the temporary obftruction
was removed, and the deluded purchafers were
fpeedily convinced of the impofition.

So grievoufly are the negroes fometimes afflicted with this troublefome and painful diforder, that
I have feen large numbers of them, after being
landed, obliged by the virulence of the complaint, to ftop almoft every minute, as they paf-
fed on.

Treatment

Treatment of the Sailors.

The evils attendant on this inhuman traffick, are not confined to the purchased negroes. The sufferings of the seamen employed in the slave-trade, from the unwholesomeness of the climate, the inconveniences of the voyage, the brutal severity of the commanders, and other causes, fall very little short, nor prove in proportion to the numbers, less destructive to the sailors than negroes.

The sailors on board the Guinea ships, are not allowed always an equal quantity of beef and pork with those belonging to other merchant ships. In these articles they are frequently much stinted, particularly when the negroes are on board; part of the stock laid in for the sailors, being, as before observed, appropriated to their use.

With regard to their drink, they are generally denied grog, and are seldom allowed any thing but water to quench their thirst. This urges them, when opportunity offers, at Bonny and other places on the coast, to barter their clothes with the natives, for English brandy, which the Africans obtain, among other articles, in exchange for slaves; and they frequently leave themselves nearly naked, in order to indulge an excess in spiritous liquors. In this state, they are often found lying on the deck, and in different parts of the ship, exposed to the heavy dews which in those climates fall during the night; notwithstanding the deck is usually washed every evening. This frequently causes pains in the head and limbs, accompanied with a

C 3 fever,

fever, which generally, in the courfe of a few days, occafion their death.

The temporary houfe conftructed on the deck, affords but an indifferent fhelter from the weather; yet the failors are obliged to lodge under it, as all the parts between decks are occupied by, or kept for, the negroes. The cabin is frequently full, and when this is the cafe, or the captain finds the heat and the ftench intolerable, he quits his cot, which is ufually hung over the flaves, and fleeps in the round-houfe, if there be one, as there is in many fhips.

The foul air that arifes from the negroes when they are much crowded, is very noxious to the crew; and this is not a little increafed by the additional heat which the covering over the fhip occafions. The mangrove fmoke is likewife, as before obferved, productive of diforders among them.

Nor are they better accommodated after they leave the Coaft of Africa. During the whole of the paffage to the Weft-Indies, which in general lafts feven weeks, or two months, they are obliged, for want of room between decks, to keep upon deck. This expofure to the weather, is alfo found very prejudicial to the health of the failors, and frequently occafions fevers, which generally prove fatal. The only refemblance of a fhelter, is a tarpawling thrown over the booms, which even before they leave the coaft, is generally fo full of holes, as to afford fcarce any defence againft the wind or the rain, of which a confiderable quantity ufually falls during this paffage.

Many other caufes contribute to affect the health of the failors. The water at Bonny, which they are obliged to drink, is very unwholefome; and,

together

together with their fcanty and bad diet, and the cruel ufage they receive from the officers, tends to impoverifh the blood, and render them extremely fufceptible of putrid fevers and dyfenteries.

The feamen, whofe health happen to be impaired, are difcharged, on the arrival of the fhips in the Weft-Indies, and as foon as they get afhore, they have recourfe to fpiritous liquors, to which they are the more prone, on account of having been denied grog, or even any liquor but water, during their being aboard; the confequence of which is, a certain and fpeedy deftruction. Numbers likewife die in the Weft-India iflands, of the fcurvy, brought on in confequence of poverty of diet, and expofure to all weathers.

I am now come to a part of the fufferings of the failors who are employed in the flave-trade, of which, for the honour of human nature, I would willingly decline giving an account; that is, the treatment they receive from their officers, which makes no inconfiderable addition to the hardfhips and ailments juft mentioned, and contributes not a little to rob the nation annually, of a confiderable number of this valuable body of men. However, as truth demands, and the occafion requires it, I will relate fome of the circumftances of this kind, which fell under my own immediate obfervation, during the feveral voyages I made in that line.

In one of thefe, I was witnefs to the following inftance of cruel ufage. Moft of the failors were treated with brutal feverity; but one in particular, a man advanced in years, experienced it in an uncommon degree. Having made fome complaint relative to his allowance of water, and this being conftrued into an infult, one of the officers feized

C 4 him,

him, and with the blows he beſtowed upon him, beat out ſeveral of his teeth. Not content with this, while the poor old man was yet bleeding, one of the iron pump-bolts was fixed in his mouth, and kept there by a piece of rope-yarn tied round his head. Being unable to ſpit out the blood which flowed from the wound, the man was al-moſt choaked, and obliged to ſwallow it. He was then tied to the rail of the quarter-deck, having declared, upon being gagged, that he would jump overboard and drown himſelf. About two hours after he was taken from the quarter-deck rail, and faſtened to the grating companion of the ſteerage, under the half deck, where he remained all night with a centinel placed over him.

A young man on board one of the ſhips, was frequently beaten in a very ſevere manner, for very trifling faults. This was done ſometimes with what is termed *a cat*, (an inſtrument of cor-rection, which conſiſts of a handle or ſtem, made of a rope three inches and a half in circumference, and about eighteen inches in length, at one of which are faſtened nine branches, or tails, compo-ſed of log line, with three or more knots upon each branch), and ſometimes he was beat with a bamboo. Being one day cruelly beaten with the latter, the poor lad, unable to endure the ſevere uſage, leaped out of one of the gun ports on the larboard ſide of the cabin, into the river. He, however, providentially eſcaped being de-voured by the ſharks, and was taken up by a canoe belonging to one of the black traders then lying along-ſide the veſſel. As ſoon as he was brought on board, he was dragged to the quarter-deck, and his head forced into a tub of water, which had

had been left there for the negroe women to wash their hands in. In this situation he was kept till he was nearly suffocated ; the person who held him, exclaiming, with the malignity of a demon, " If you want drowning, I will drown you myself." Upon my inquiring of the young man, if he knew the danger to which he exposed himself by jumping overboard, he replied, " that he expected to " be devoured by the sharks, but he preferred " even that, to being treated daily with so much " cruelty."

Another seaman having been in some degree negligent, had a long chain fixed round his neck, at the end of which was fastened a log of wood. In this situation he performed his duty, (from which he was not in the least spared) for several weeks, till at length he was nearly exhausted by fatigue ; and after his release from the log, he was frequently beaten for trivial faults. Once, in particular, when an accident happened, through the carelesness of another seaman, he was tied up, although the fault was not in the least imputable to him, along with the other person, and they were both flogged till their backs were raw. Chian pepper was then mixed in a bucket, with salt water, and with this the harrowed parts of the back of the unoffending seaman were washed, as an addition to his torture.

The same seaman having at another time accidentally broken a plate, a fish-gig was thrown at him with great violence. The fish-gig is an instrument used for striking fish, and consists of several strong barbed points fixed on a pole, about six feet long, loaded at the end with lead. The man escaped the threatening danger, by stooping his head, and the missile weapon struck in the barricado.

cado. Knives and forks were at other times thrown at him; and a large Newfoundland dog was frequently set at him, which, thus encouraged, would not only tear his cloths, but wound him. At length, after several severe floggings, and other ill treatment, the poor fellow appeared to be totally insensible to beating, and careless of the event.

I must here add, that whenever any of the crew were beaten, the Newfoundland dog, just mentioned, from the encouragement he met with, would generally leap upon them, tear their cloths, and bite them. He was particularly inveterate against one of the seamen, who, from being often knocked down, and severely beaten, appeared quite stupid, and incapable of doing his duty. In this state, he was taken on board another ship, and returned to England.

In one of my voyages, a seaman came on board the ship I belonged to, while on the coast, as a passenger to the West-Indies. He was just recovered from a fever, and notwithstanding this, he was very unmercifully beaten during the passage, which, together with the feeble state he was in at the time, rendered him nearly incapable of walking, and it was but by stealth, that any medical assistance could be given to him.

A young man was likewise beaten and kicked almost daily, for trifling, and even imaginary faults. The poor youth happening to have a very bad toe, through a hurt, he was placed as a centry over the sick slaves, a station which required much walking. This, in addition to the pain it occasioned, increased a fever he already had. Soon after he was compelled, although so ill, to sit on the gratings, and being there overcome with illness and fatigue,

he

he chanced to fall afleep; which being obferved from the quarter-deck, he was foon awakened, and with many oaths, upbraided for neglect of duty. He was then kicked from the gratings, and fo cruelly beaten, that it was with great difficulty he crawled to one of the officers who was more humane, and complaining of the cruel treatment he had juft received, petitioned for a little barley-water (which was kept for the fick flaves) to quench the intolerable thirft he experienced.

Another feaman was knocked down feveral times a day, for faults of no deep dye. It being obferved at one time, that the hen coops had not been removed by the failors who were then wafhing the deck, nor wafhed under, which it was his duty to fee done, one of the officers immediately knocked him down, then feized and dragged him to the ftern of the veffel, where he threw him violently againft the deck. By this treatment, various parts of his body was much bruifed, his face fwelled, and he had a bad eye for a fortnight. He was afterwards feverely beaten for a very trifling fault, and kicked till he fell down. When he got on fhore in the Weft-Indies, he carried his fhirt, ftained with the blood which had flowed from his wounds, to one of the magiftrates of the ifland, and applied to him for redrefs; but the fhip being configned to one of them, all the redrefs he could procure, was his difcharge.

Many other inftances of fimilar feverity might be produced; but the foregoing will fuffice, to give fome idea of the treatment feamen are liable to, and generally experience, in this employ; the confequence of which ufually is defertion or death.

Of

Of the former I will give one inftance. While
a fhip I belonged to lay at Bonny, early one
morning near a dozen of the crew deferted in one
of the long boats. They were driven to this
defperate meafure, as one of them afterwards informed me, by the cruel treatment they had experienced on board. Two of them, in particular,
had been feverely beaten and flogged the preceding day. One of thefe having neglected to fee
that the arms of the fhip were kept fit for ufe,
was tied up to the mizen fhrouds, and after
being ftripped, very feverely flogged on the back;
his trowfers were then pulled down, and the flog-
ing was repeated. The other feaman, who was
efteemed a careful, cleanly, fober fellow, had been
punifhed little lefs feverely, though it did not
appear that he had been guilty at that time of
any fault.

It is cuftomary for moft of the captains of the
flave fhips to go on fhore every evening to do
bufinefs with the black traders. Upon thefe occafions many of them get intoxicated, and when
they return on board, give proofs of their inebria-
tion, by beating and ill ufing fome or other of the
crew. This was the prefent cafe; the feaman here
fpoken of, was beaten, without any reafon being
affigned, with a knotted bamboo, for a confiderable time; by which he was very much bruifed,
and being before in an ill ftate of health, fuffered
confiderably.

Irritated by the ill ufage which all of them, in
their turn, had experienced, they refolved to attempt an efcape, and effected it early in the
morning. The perfon on the watch difcovered,
that the net-work on the main deck had been cut,
and that one of the long-boats was gone; and,
upon

upon farther examination it was found, that near a dozen of the feamen were miffing. A few hours after, the captain went in the cutter in purfuit of the deferters, but without fuccefs.

On my return to England, I received from one of them, the following account of their adventures during this undertaking.

When they left the veffel, they propofed going to Old Calabar, being determined to perifh, rather than return to the fhip. All the provifions they took with them was, a bag containing about half a hundred weight of bread, half a fmall cheefe, and a cafk of water of about 38 gallons. They made a fail of a hammock, and erected one of the boat's oars for a maft. Thus flenderly provided, they dropped down the river of Bonny, and kept along the coaft; but miftaking one river for another, they were feized by the natives, who ftripped them, and marched them acrofs the country, for a confiderable diftance, to the place to which they themfelves intended going. During the march, feveral were taken ill, and fome of them died. Thofe who furvived, were fold to an Engiifh fhip which lay there. Every one of thefe deferters, except three, died on the coaft, or during their paffage to the Weft-Indies; and one of the remaining three died foon after his arrival there. So that only two out of the whole number, lived to arrive in England, and thofe in a very infirm ftate of health.

While I am upon the fubject of the defertions among the failors, I muft add, that the captains in this trade generally take out with them tobacco and flops, which they fell at an exorbitant price to the failors. And in cafe of their defertion or deceafe, they have it in their power to charge to the

the feamens accounts, whatever quantity they pleafe, without contradiction. This proves an additional reafon for cruel ufage. In cafe of defertion, the failors forfeit their wages, by which the expences of the voyage are leffened, and confequently the merchants reap benefit from it.

The relation juft given of the barbarities exercifed by the officers in the flave trade, upon the feamen under their command, may appear to thofe who are unacquainted with the method in which this iniquitous branch of commerce is conducted, to be exaggerated. But I can affure them, that every inftance is confined within the ftricteft bounds of truth. Many others may likewife be brought to prove, that thofe I have recited are by no means fingular. Indeed, the reverfe of this conduct would be efteemed a fingularity. For the common practice of the officers in the Guinea trade, I am forry to fay it, will, with a very few exceptions, juftify the affertion, that to harden the feelings, and to infpire a *delight in giving torture* to a fellow creature, is the natural tendency of this unwarrantable traffick. It is but juftice however, that I except from this general cenfure, one captain with whom I failed. Upon all occafions I found him to be a humane and confiderate man, and ever ready to alleviate the evils attendant on the trade, as far as they were to be leffened.

The annual diminution of Britifh feamen by all the foregoing caufes, is what next claims attention, and upon due inveftigation will be found, I fear, to be much more confiderable than it is generally fuppofed to be. As this is a queftion of great national importance, and cannot fail to evince the neceffity of an abolition of the

flave

flave trade; in order to convey to the public fome
idea of the deftructive tendency of it, I will give
an account of the ftatement of the lofs of a fhip, to
which I belonged, during one of her voyages.
And though this ftatement may not be confider-
ed as an average of the lofs upon each voyage,
which I have before eftimated, as I would not wifh
to exceed the mark, at one fourth, and oftentimes
one third. I have known inftances where it has
been greatly exceeded, as I fhall prefently fhew.

The crew of the fhip I fpeak of, upon its departure from England, confifted of forty-fix perfons, exclufive of the captain, chief mate, and
myfelf. Out of this number, we loft on the coaft
eleven by defertion (of whom only two, and thofe
in a very infirm ftate, ever arrived in England)
and five by death. Three perifhed in the middle
paffage, of whom one was a paffenger. In the
Weft-Indies, two died, one of which was a paffenger from Bonny. Five were difcharged at their
own requeft, having been cruelly treated, and five
deferted, exclufive of two who fhipped themfelves
at Bonny; of thefe ten, feveral were in a difeafed
ftate; and probably, like moft of the feamen who
are difcharged or defert from the Guinea fhips in
the iflands, never returned to their native country. One died in our paffage from the Weft-Indies to England; and one, having been rendered
incapable of duty, was fent on board another
fhip while we lay at Bonny.

Thus, out of the forty-fix perfons before-mentioned, only fifteen returned home in the fhip.
And feveral, out of this fmall number, fo ener-
vated in their conftitution, as to be of little fer-
vice in future; they were, on the contrary, reduced to the mournful neceffity of becoming
burthenfome

burthenſome to themſelves and to others. Of the ten that deſerted, or were diſcharged in the Weſt-Indies, little account can be taken; it being extremely improbable that one half, perhaps not a third, ever returned to this country.

From hence it appears, that there was a loſs in this voyage of thirty-one ſailors and upwards, excluſive of the two ſailors who were paſſengers, and not included in the ſhip's crew. I ſay *a loſs of thirty-one*, for though the whole of this number did not die, yet if it be conſidered, that ſeveral of thoſe who returned to England in the ſhip, or who might have returned by other ſhips, are likely to become a burthen, inſtead of being uſeful to the community, it will be readily acknowledged, I doubt not, that the foregoing ſtatement does not exceed reality.

How worthy of ſerious conſideration is the diminution here repreſented, of a body of people ſo valuable in a commercial ſtate! But how much more alarming will this be, when it appears, as is really the caſe, that the loſs of ſeamen in the voyage I am ſpeaking of, is not equal to what is experienced even by ſome other ſhips trading to Bonny and Calabar; and much leſs than by thoſe employed in boating on the Windward Coaſt; where frequently there happens ſuch a mortality among the crew, as not to leave a ſufficient number of hands to navigate the ſhips to the Weſt-Indies. In the year 1786, I ſaw a ſhip, belonging to Miles Barber, and Co. at Cape Monſerado, on the Windward Coaſt, which had loſt all the crew except three, from *boating*; a practice that proves extremely deſtructive to ſailors, by expoſing them to the parching ſun and heavy dews of Africa, for weeks together, while they

are

are seeking for negroes up the rivers, as before described.

It might naturally be afked, as fuch are the dangers to which the failors employed in the flave trade are expofed from the intemperature of the climate, the inconveniencies of the voyage, and the treatment of the officers, how the captains are able to procure a fufficient number to man their fhips. I anfwer, that it is done by a feries of fineffe and impofition, aided not only by allurements, but by threats.

There are certain public-houfes, in which, for interefted purpofes, the failors are trufted, and encouraged to run in debt. To the landlords of thefe houfes the captains apply. And a certain number being fixed on, the landlord immediately infifts upon their entering on board fuch a fhip, threatening, in cafe of refufal, to arreft and throw them into prifon. At the fame time the captain holds out the allurements of a month's pay in advance above the fhips in any other trade, and the promife of fatisfying their inexorable landlords. Thus terrified on the one hand by the apprehenfions of a prifon, and allured on the other by the promifed advance, they enter. And by this means a very great proportion of the failors in the flave trade are procured; only a very fmall number of landmen are employed. During the feveral voyages I have been in the trade, I have not known the number to exceed one for each voyage. The few fhips that go out in time of war, generally take with them, as other merchant fhips do, a greater proportion of landmen. And with regard to apprentices, we had not any on board the

D   fhips

ships I failed in, neither to my knowledge have I ever seen any. So far is this trade from proving a nursery for seamen.

By their articles, on entering on board some Guinea ships, the sailors are restrained, under forfeiture of their wages, from applying, in case of ill usage, to any one for redress, except to such persons as shall be nominated by the owners or the captain; and by others, to commence an action against the captain for bad treatment, incurs a penalty of fifty pounds. These restrictions seem to be a tacit acknowledgment on the part of the owners and captains, that ill treatment is to be expected.

Having stated the foregoing facts relative to the nature of this destructive and inhuman traffick, I shall leave those, whose more immediate business it is, to deduce the necessary conclusions; and shall proceed to give a few cursory observations on those parts of the coast of Africa already referred to; confining myself to such as tend to an elucidation of the slave trade, without entering minutely into the state of the country.

A short

A short Description of such Parts of the Coast of Guinea, as are before referred to.

BONNY, or BANNY, is a large town situate in the Bight of Benin, on the coast of Guinea, lying about twelve miles from the sea, on the east side of a river of the same name, opposite to a town called Peterforte-side. It consists of a considerable number of very poor huts, built of upright poles, plaistered with a kind of red earth, and covered with mats. They are very low, being only one story. The floor is made of sand, which being constructed on swampy ground, does not long retain its firmness, but requires frequent repair.

The inhabitants secure themselves, in some degree, against the noxious vapours, which arise from the swamps and woods that surround the town, by constantly keeping large wood fires in their huts. They are extremely dirty and indolent ; which, together with what they call the *smokes*, (a noxious vapour, arising from the swamps about the latter end of autumn) produces an epidemical fever, that carries off great numbers.

The natives of Bonny believe in one Supreme Being ; but they reverence greatly a harmless animal of the lizard kind, called a Guana, the body of which is about the size of a man's leg, and tapering towards its tail, nearly to a point. Great numbers of them run about the town, being encouraged and cherished by the inhabitants.

The

The river of Bonny abounds with sharks of a
very large size, which are often seen in almost
incredible numbers about the slave ships, devour-
ing with great dispatch the dead bodies of the
negroes as they are thrown overboard. The bodies of the sailors who die there, are buried on a
sandy point, called Bonny Point, which lies about
a quarter of a mile from the town. It is covered
at high water; and, as the bodies are buried but
a small depth below the surface of the sand, the
stench arising from them is sometimes very noxious.

The trade of this town consists of slaves, and a
small quantity of ivory and palm-oil, the latter of
which the inhabitants use as we do butter; but
its chief dependence is on the slave trade, in
which it exceeds any other place on the coast of
Africa. The only water here is rain-water, which
stagnating in a dirty pool, is very unwholesome.
With this, as there is no better to be procured,
the ships are obliged to supply themselves, though,
when drank by the sailors, it frequently occasions
violent pains in the bowels, accompanied with a
diarrhœa.

THE WINDWARD COAST of Africa has a very
beautiful appearance from the sea, being covered
with trees, which are green all the year. It produces rice, cotton, and indigo of the first quality,
and likewise a variety of roots, such as yams,
casava, sweet potatoes, &c. &c. The soil is very
rich, and the rice which it produces, is superior
to that of Carolina; the cotton also is very fine.
It has a number of fine rivers, that are navigable
for small sloops, a considerable way up the country.

The

The natives are a strong hardy race, especially about Setrecrou, where they are always employed in hunting and fishing. They are extremely athletic and muscular, and are very expert in the water, and can swim for many miles. They can likewise dive to almost any depth. I have often thrown pieces of iron and tobacco pipes overboard, which they have never failed bringing up in their hand.

Their canoes are very small, not weighing above twenty-eight pounds each, and seldom carrying above two or three people. It is surprizing to see with what rapidity they paddle themselves through the water, and to what a distance they venture in them from the shore. I have seen them eight or nine miles distant from it. In stormy weather the sea frequently fills them, which the persons in them seem to disregard. When this happens, they leap into the sea, and taking hold of the ends of the canoe, turn her over several times, till they have emptied her of the chief part of the water; they then get in again, with great agility, and throw out the remainder with a small scoop, made for that purpose.

They sell some ivory and Malegetta pepper.

They are very cleanly in their houses, as likewise in cooking their victuals. The ivory on this coast is very fine, especially at Cape Lahoe. There are on this coast small cattle.

The Gold Coast has not so pleasing an appearance from the sea, as the Windward coast; but the natives are full as hardy, if not more so. The reason given for this is, that as their country is not so fertile as the Windward Coast, they are obliged to labour more in the cultivation of rice and corn, which is their chief food. They have
here,

here, as on the Windward Coaſt, hogs, goats, fowls, and abundance of fine fiſh, &c. They are very fond of brandy, and always get intoxicated when it is in their power to do ſo. They are like-wiſe very bold and reſolute, and inſurrections hap-pen more frequently among them, when on ſhip-board, than amongſt the negroes of any other part of the coaſt.

The trade here is carried on by means of gold-duſt, for which the Europeans give them goods, ſuch as pieces of India chintz, bafts, romals, guns, powder, tobacco, brandy, pewter, iron, lead, cop-per, knives, &c. &c. After the gold duſt is pur-chaſed, it is again diſpoſed of to the natives for negroes. Their mode of reckoning in this traffick, is by ounces; thus they ſay they will have ſo many ounces for a ſlave; and according to the number of ſhips on the coaſt, the price of theſe differs.

The Engliſh have ſeveral forts on the Gold Coaſt, the principle of which are, Cape Corſe, and Anamaboe. The trade carried on at theſe forts, is bartering for negroes, which the governors ſell again to the European ſhips, for the articles before-mentioned.

The natives, as juſt obſerved, are a bold, reſolute people. During the laſt voyage I was upon the coaſt, I ſaw a number of negroes in Cape Corſe Caſtle, ſome of whom were part of the cargo of a ſhip from London, on whoſe crew they had riſen, and, after killing the captain and moſt of the ſailors, ran the ſhip on ſhore; but in endeavour-ing to make their eſcape, moſt of them were ſeized by the natives, and reſold. Eighteen of theſe we purchaſed from Governor Morgue. The Dutch have likewiſe a ſtrong fort on this coaſt, called Elmina,

Elmina, where they carry on a confiderable trade for flaves.

The principal places of trade for negroes, are Bonny and Calabar. The town and trade of Bonny, I have already defcribed. That of Calabar is nearly fimilar. The natives of the latter are of a much more delicate frame than thofe of the Windward and Gold Coafts.

The natives of Angola are the mildeft, and moft expert in mechanicks, of any of the Africans. Their country is the moft plentiful of any in thofe parts, and produces different forts of grain, particularly calavances, of which they feem, when on fhip-board, to be extremely fond. Here are likewife hogs, fheep, goats, fowls, &c. in great abundance, infomuch, that when I was at the River Ambris, we could buy a fine fat fheep for a fmall keg of gunpowder, the value of which was about one fhilling and fixpence fterling. They have alfo great plenty of fine fifh. I have often feen turtle caught, while fifhing with a net for other fifh. They have a fpecies of wild cinnamon, which has a very pungent tafte in the mouth. The foil feems extremely rich, and the vegetation luxuriant and quick. A perfon might walk for miles in the country amidft wild jeffamin trees.

The Portuguefe have a large town on this coaft, named St. Paul's, the inhabitants of which, and of the country for many miles round, profefs the Roman Catholick religion. They are in general ftrictly honeft. The town of St. Paul's is ftrongly fortified, and the Portuguefe do not fuffer any other nation to trade there.

THE END.

BOOKS lately Publiſhed by JAMES PHILLIPS, George-Yard, Lombard-Street.

ESSAY on the Treatment and Converſion of African Slaves in the Britiſh Sugar Colonies. By the Rev. J. RAMSAY, Vicar of Teſton in Kent. 4s. Boards.

An INQUIRY into the Effects of putting a Stop to the African Slave Trade, and of granting Liberty to the Slaves in the Britiſh Sugar Colonies. By J. RAMSAY. 6d.

A REPLY to the Perſonal Invectives and Objections contained in Two Anſwers, publiſhed by certain anonymous Perſons, to an Eſſay on the Treatment and Converſion of African Slaves, in the Britiſh Colonies. By JAMES RAMSAY. 2s.

A LETTER from Capt. J. S. SMITH, to the Rev. Mr. HILL, on the State of the Negroe Slaves. To which are added an Introduction, and Remarks on Free Negroes. By the EDITOR. 6d.

A CAUTION to Great Britain and her Colonies, in a ſhort Repreſentation of the calamitous State of the enſlaved Negroes in the Britiſh Dominions. By ANTHONY BENEZET. 6d.

The CASE of our Fellow-Creatures, the Oppreſſed Africans, reſpectfully recommended to the ſerious Conſideration of the Legiſlature of Great Britain, by the People called Quakers. 2d.

A Summary View of the SLAVE TRADE, and of the probable Conſequences of its Abolition. 2d.

A LETTER to the Treaſurer of the Society inſtituted for the Purpoſe of effecting the Abolition of the SLAVE TRADE. From the Rev. ROBERT BOUCHER NICKOLLS, Dean of Middleham. 2d.

A new and much enlarged Edition of CLARKSON's ESSAYS will ſoon be publiſhed.